Raising Grandpa

Coping For Kids

Alzheimer's

Lucinda
Moebius

Illustrated by Carrie
Nawrocki

Haven Novels 2014

Haven Novels

Boise ID 83713

www.lucindamoebius.com

First Hardcover Edition: 2014

First Paperback Edition: 2014

First E-Book Edition: 2014

Raising Grandpa

a book by Lucinda Moebius. -1st. ed. p.cm.

ISBN-13:9780692317129

Cover design by: Carrie Nawrocki

Illustrations by: Carrie Nawrocki

Printed in the United States of America

Haven Novels

Raising Grandpa

Coping For Kids
Alzheimer's

by

Lucinda Moebius

Masters of Education, Ed.D Candidate

Illustrated by
Carrie Nawrocki

Secondary education, Bachelor of Science

Family   Love

My name is Sammy and I live with my Momma and Daddy and my brother Billy and now my Grandpa. Grandpa moved into my old room.

Momma and Daddy had to do lots of work to get it ready for him. He even has a special bed to keep him safe.

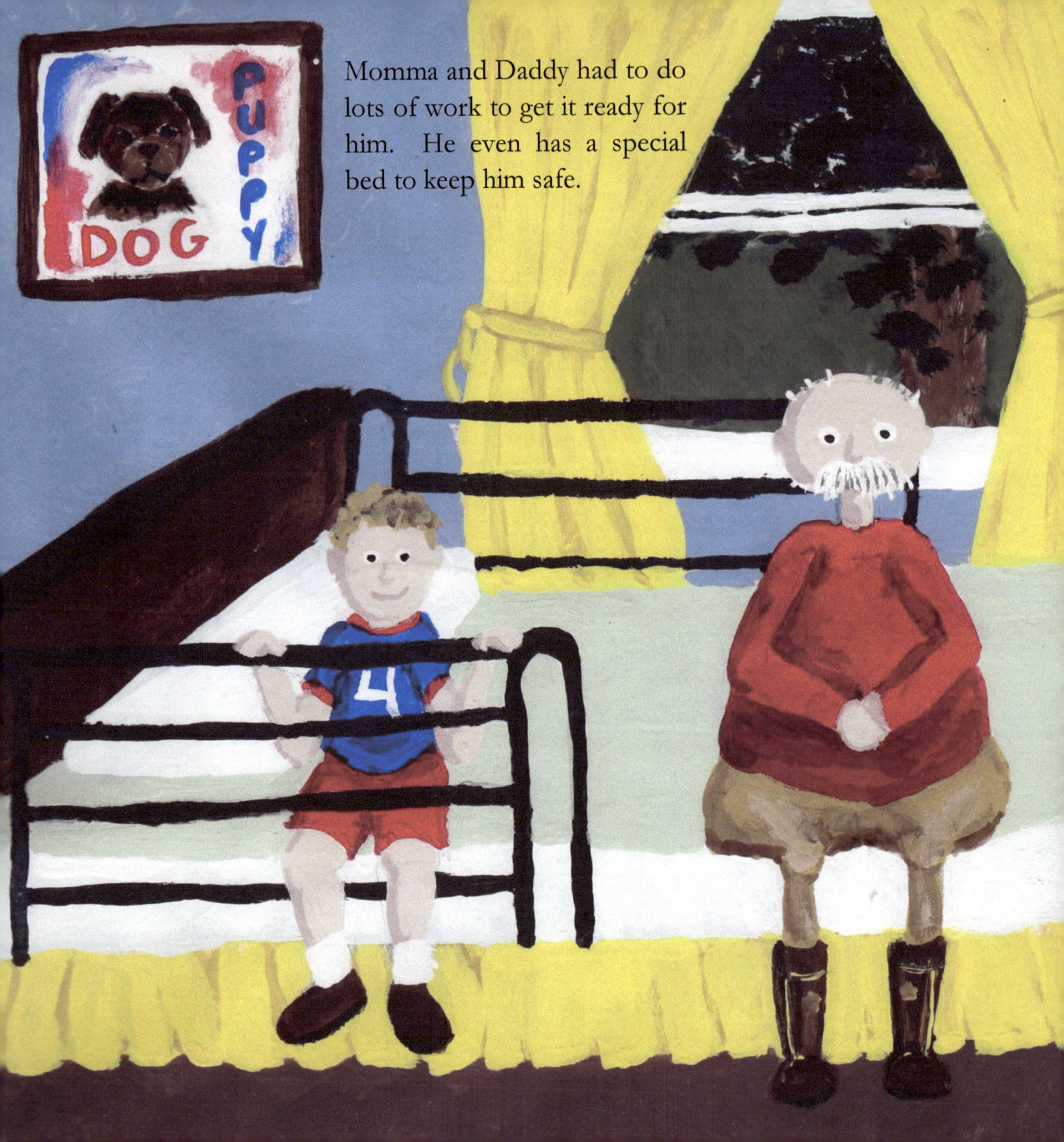

DOG PUPPY

I moved in to my older brother Billy's room. His room is always messy. I can never find my toys when I want to play.

Momma says we have to work hard to keep Grandpa safe. She is afraid he will take a walk and get lost. He did that a lot when he lived in his old house. Getting lost makes me afraid. It must make him afraid, too. Grandpa and me like to take walks together. It's my favorite Grandpa time.

FAMILY

Momma says to be extra careful and keep our toys and clothes out of the hallway because Grandpa can't see very good anymore and has problems picking up his feet. She doesn't want him to fall and get hurt.

Momma says Grandpa has something called Alzheimer's. It's a hard word to say right. Like Alts-hime-ers. I don't know what it means. I think it's like becoming a kid again because sometimes Momma sighs and says she feels like she's raising three boys instead of two. She says she's raising Grandpa.

Momma used to play with me all the time.
Now, when I ask, she always says no. She
has to take care of Grandpa. It makes me
sad when Momma can't play with me.
Helping Grandpa takes lots of work.

Grandpa likes to try to make snacks in the kitchen. Most of the time he just makes a mess. When he makes snacks at night it makes Momma extra tired and grumpy in the morning.

Momma took all the knobs off the stove and put locks on the cabinets in the kitchen. I think this made Grandpa mad because he yelled really loud and I got scared.

When Grandpa gets mad Billy and me go play in our room or outside in the yard until Momma talks to him and calms him down.

Momma says it's hard for Grandpa to control his anger and we have to be careful not to upset him. When I get mad I get put in timeout. I don't think it's very fair. Grandpa should be put in timeout, too.

I like it when Grandpa plays with us even though he sometimes calls me Jake instead of Sammy. Momma says he calls me Jake because he gets confused and thinks it's forty years ago when Uncle Jake was a little boy.

Uncle Jake and Grandpa

I don't care when he calls me Jake because I know he loves me and he rubs my head, but Momma says we need to remind Grandpa my name is Sammy and I'm his grandson. Momma calls it "keeping him grounded".

When Grandpa has what Momma calls his good days she sits on the couch with him looking at pictures and listening to his stories. She writes down the stories and puts them in a memory book with the pictures. I sit with them and look at the pictures, too. I like Grandpa's stories.

My favorite story is the one of Momma running through the sprinkler in her underwear when she was a kid like me. When I tried to do the same thing Momma made me put on a pair of shorts. Grandpa laughed and laughed and I ran up to him and gave him a big, wet hug.

hunting.
ime. Your
watched
ed all
scared us
!

ME & MOM

Ladies come to our house and help almost every day. Momma calls them angels. I don't see wings on them, but they really help Momma, especially on Grandpa's bad days.

They help him bathe and eat and change his clothes and clean his room. I wish they would help me with my chores. Usually Grandpa likes it when they help him, but sometimes he gets angry and yells and tries to push them away. The ladies are really good at talking to Grandpa and calming him down.

I think Momma gets confused sometimes because instead of angels she calls the ladies caregivers. I just think they are really neat because when they make Grandpa a snack they always give me one too. Grandpa and me sit at the table and eat snacks together.

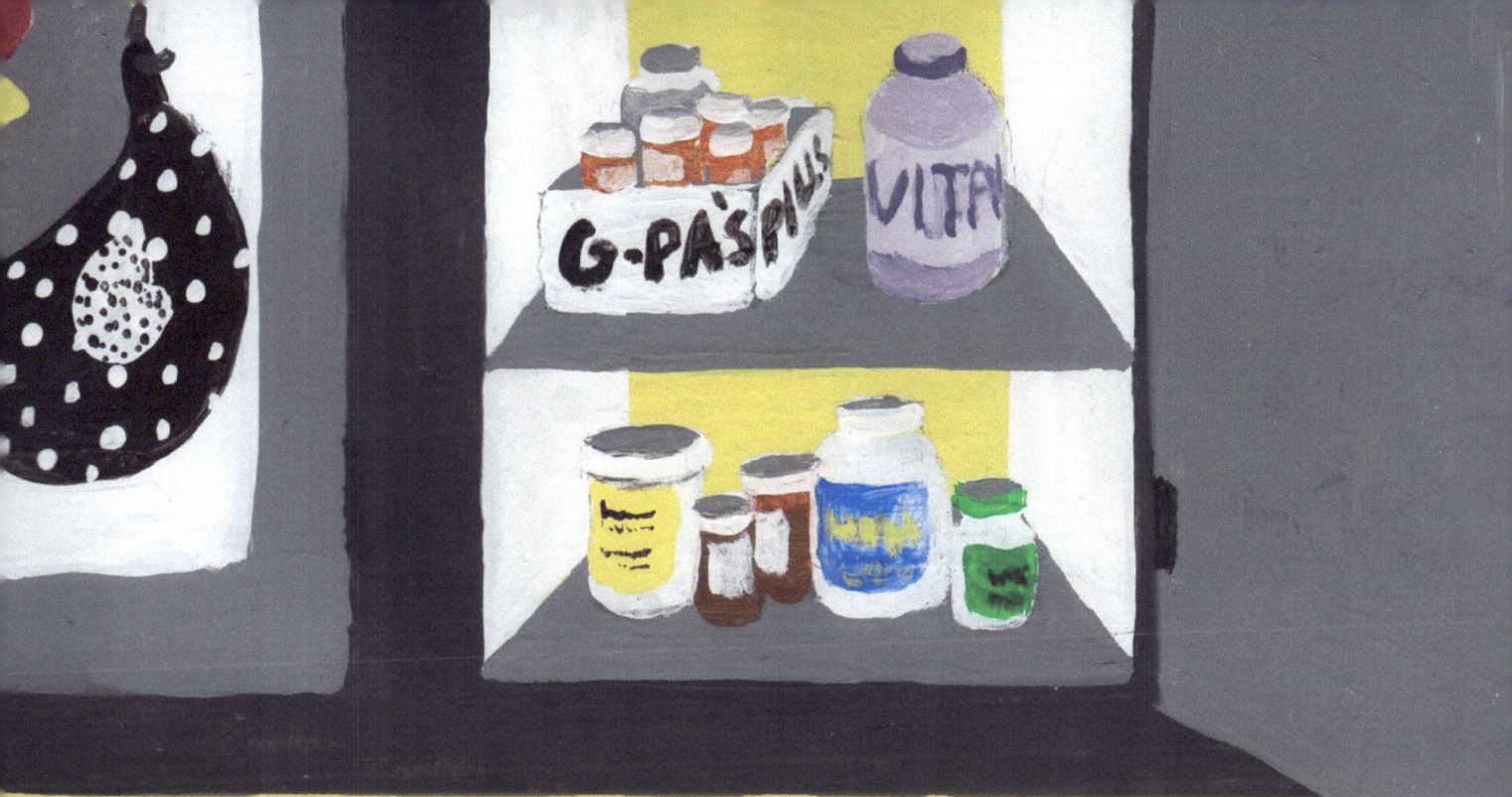

The ladies also help Grandpa with his medicine. Grandpa takes lots of medicine. No one is allowed to touch it except Momma and Daddy and the ladies. They keep it locked in the cabinet with mine and Billy's vitamins and Momma's headache medicine.

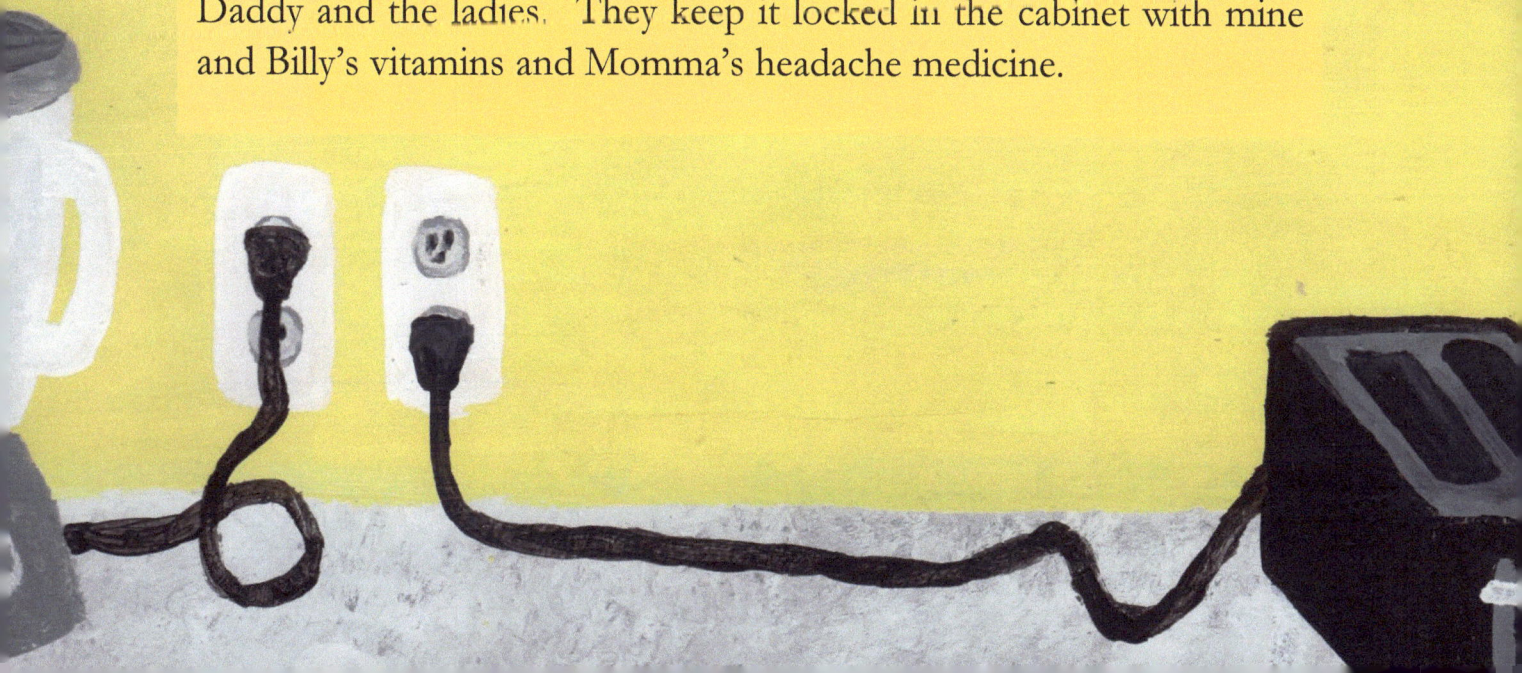

Together Forever

Momma says Grandpa isn't going to be able to live with us forever, but we need to be patient and take care of him as long as we can. She says we are a family and families take care of each other. It's just what we do.

I like my family.

Even though my brother is messy and Grandpa gets confused. We all love each other very much. I'm glad Grandpa moved into my room.

www.ingramcontent.com/pod-product-compliance
Lightning Source LLC
Chambersburg PA
CBHW042112040426

42448CB00002B/241